Teens and OCD

Barbara Sheen

ReferencePoint Press®

San Diego, CA

© 2017 ReferencePoint Press, Inc.
Printed in the United States

For more information, contact:
ReferencePoint Press, Inc.
PO Box 27779
San Diego, CA 92198
www.ReferencePointPress.com

LIBRARY OF CONGRESS CATALOGING-IN-PUBLICATION DATA

Names: Sheen, Barbara, author.
Title: Teens and OCD / by Barbara Sheen.
Description: San Diego, CA : ReferencePoint Press, Inc., 2017. | Series: Teen
  mental health series | Audience: Grade 9 to 12. | Includes bibliographical
  references and index.
Identifiers: LCCN 2016034107 (print) | LCCN 2016035642 (ebook) | ISBN
  9781682821268 (hardback) | ISBN 9781682821275 (eBook)
Subjects: LCSH: Obsessive-compulsive disorder in adolescence. |
  Obsessive-compulsive disorder in adolescence--Treatment.
Classification: LCC RJ506.O25 S54 2017 (print) | LCC RJ506.O25 (ebook) | DDC
  616.85/22700835--dc23
LC record available at https://lccn.loc.gov/2016034107

CONTENTS

A Misunderstood Disorder

Morgan is a college student and a blogger on mental health issues. She has obsessive-compulsive disorder (OCD). As a child she was plagued with obsessions—distressing, repetitive thoughts—that her family would die while she was sleeping. These thoughts so frightened her that, before going to bed each night, she repeatedly knocked on wood in multiples of threes until she reached what she considered a safe number. This ritual, or compulsive behavior, took about an hour to complete. She believed that if she did not do the ritual her family would die, but if she performed the ritual correctly, her family would live through the night. Performing the ritual gave her a temporary feeling of relief. Soon, though, her distressing thoughts returned and she found herself doing more complex and time-consuming rituals to protect her loved ones and ease her anxiety. "All of this responsibility was very confusing," she confesses. "Why was I so dangerous? Why could only I save them? Why weren't these thoughts and rituals my choice?"[1]

Over the years the content and severity of Morgan's obsessions changed. When one fear disappeared, another one replaced it. And old fears often returned. She was aware that her thoughts were irrational, but that did not make them any less scary. Indeed, her fear was so intense that she felt forced to perform rituals to ease her mind. As the Mayo Clinic explains, "With OCD, you may . . . realize that your obsessions aren't reasonable, and you may try to ignore them or stop them. But that only increases your distress and anxiety. Ultimately, you feel driven to perform compulsive acts in an effort to ease your stressful feelings."[2]

By the time Morgan entered college, obsessive thoughts and compulsive acts were eating up more and more of her time. She spent hours performing mental and physical rituals to lower her anxiety and keep bad things from happening. As she explains,

> Everything you do takes longer than it should. . . . Starting from the second you wake up. First, when choosing what to wear better not wear anything blue or something bad will happen. Next, be sure to unplug everything in sight before you leave and tap the light switch just right or the whole building will burst into flames. Next, you better not go anywhere without a water bottle or you will die. Next, when doing homework reread that sentence two, five, ten, fifteen times even if it takes an hour to read a few pages, so you absolutely do not miss any information. Next, allot at least an hour to get ready for bed. With enough useless rituals it can easily take that long. Next, spend fifteen minutes checking you set your alarm clock, otherwise you may miss class and will be hated.[3]

Hiding Fears and Rituals

Despite being afflicted with distressing obsessions and compulsive rituals, like many people with OCD, Morgan kept her illness secret for years. OCD symptoms are often strange. Many people with OCD feel ashamed of their thoughts and behavior. They worry that if others knew about their condition, they would be labeled as bad, weird, or crazy. Consequently, many OCD sufferers work hard to hide their symptoms.

This is especially true for teenagers who want to be accepted by their peers. For adolescents, being different can be socially unacceptable; to keep from being judged unfairly, many teens with OCD hide their disorder. In his book *The Ray of Hope*, Ray St. John, a teenager with OCD, writes, "We OCDers are extraordinarily good at hiding our symptoms. We know that our

Teens with OCD often hide their symptoms because they fear that others will think them crazy, bad, or just plain weird. Suffering in silence not only prevents them from getting help but also adds to their anxiety.

obsessions are not grounded in reality and that our compulsions do nothing but temporarily relieve our anxieties. We know that our thinking and our actions are weird. And, we go to extreme lengths to hide their weirdness from our friends, teachers, employers, and even certain family members."[4]

Hiding OCD symptoms is physically and emotionally taxing. Moreover, it can keep individuals from getting the help they need. According to Alison Dotson, an author and the president of OCD Twin Cities, in Minnesota, "It can take years for someone with OCD to get the right help, and not because psychiatrists and therapists don't know what to do. Rather, it's because we don't seek it out. I was so sure I would be judged that I didn't make an appointment with a psychiatrist until I was 26 years old—and I have been obsessed for well over a decade."[5]

A Misunderstood Condition

Individuals with OCD are not alone in misunderstanding the disorder. Misconceptions about OCD are common. In fact, it is often depicted in the media as a humorous personality quirk; in reality, though, it is a serious mental disorder.

Lack of understanding about OCD can be especially hard for teenagers. In some cases, when they reveal their problem, misinformed family members blame teens for not taking control of their symptoms and stopping their odd behavior. As Molly, a nineteen-year-old with OCD confesses, "There are many stereotypes about OCD, one of them being that we are faking or causing it ourselves. My parents never understood this disorder and always thought it was in my head. . . . If I knew when I was 15 years old what I know now, my entire life would have been different."[6]

Learning more about OCD is one of the best ways to destroy erroneous beliefs. Greater understanding of OCD can help teens with the disorder to overcome damaging self-perceptions. It can help their family and friends to provide them with support and understanding. As a result, teens with OCD should be more comfortable opening up to a mental health professional and getting the help they need.

"We OCDers are extraordinarily good at hiding our symptoms. . . . We know that our thinking and our actions are weird. And, we go to extreme lengths to hide their weirdness from our friends, teachers, employers, and even certain family members."[4]

—Ray St. John, a young man with OCD

CHAPTER ONE

What Is OCD?

Obsessive-compulsive disorder is a type of anxiety disorder. There are a number of different anxiety disorders. Each has specific symptoms. However, all anxiety disorders share a common trait: they are mental disorders that cause persistent, intense anxiety.

Teens and others with OCD are plagued with obsessions—repetitive, upsetting, unwanted thoughts, urges, and images that are often frightening or bizarre—that cause them severe anxiety. Sufferers do not want to have these thoughts, but they have difficulty stopping them. Obsessions are hard to control and can interfere with normal thoughts, making it difficult for individuals to think about anything else. Clinical psychologist Patrick B. McGrath explains that "one way people with OCD attempt to get rid of a thought is to suppress it—they tell themselves not to think it, or they try to ignore it. Unfortunately, this is often as unsuccessful as trying to get a song out of your head that you have been singing all day by trying not to think about it."[7] In an attempt to reduce the effect of obsessions and thereby ease their distress, people with OCD perform rituals, which experts call compulsive behaviors. These can be behavioral rituals, like excessive hand washing, or they can be mental rituals, such as silently counting or praying incessantly. Some people with OCD experience only obsessions or only compulsive behaviors, but this is rare. In any case, coping with OCD interferes with a person's daily life. According to the National Institutes of Health, people with OCD spend a minimum of one hour a day dealing with obsessions and compulsive acts. In severe cases, however, dealing with the disorder can take considerably more time. As psychotherapist

Jon Hershfield explains in an online interview, "The average OCD sufferer would probably be reading this . . . going, 'An hour? That sounds nice.'"[8]

Not Ordinary Worries and Actions

Obsessions and compulsions are not the same as ordinary thoughts, worries, habits, superstitions, or rituals. Ordinary worries usually relate to things that are going on in a person's life and change as events change. For instance, it is normal for teens to worry about an upcoming test. But such worries are fleeting. Once the test is over, most teens are able to put it out of their minds and think about other things. Teens with OCD, on the other hand, have trouble letting go of their worries. Once the test is over, they might spend hours retaking it in their minds, pondering every answer they gave or could have given, or agonizing over whether they remembered to put their name on their paper. Teens with OCD are no more likely to do poorly on a test or forget to put their name on their paper than their non-OCD peers. But when teens with OCD have such a thought, it is almost impossible for them to shake it off no matter how badly they want to do so. Instead, the thought plagues the teen. It keeps recurring, and each time it returns it stirs up intense feelings of fear and distress. As an article on the mental health website HealthyPlace.com comments, "Imagine your mind getting stuck on a certain image or thought. Now imagine that this image or thought plays in your mind over and over and over again. No matter what you do, it still keeps coming. You want it to stop, but it simply will not. It feels like a devastating landslide or avalanche."[9]

> "One way people with OCD attempt to get rid of a thought is to suppress it—they tell themselves not to think it, or they try to ignore it. Unfortunately, this is often as unsuccessful as trying to get a song out of your head that you have been singing all day by trying not to think about it."[7]
>
> —Patrick B. McGrath, director of the OCD and Related Anxiety Disorders Program at the Alexian Brothers Behavioral Health Hospital in Hoffman Estates, Illinois

In an attempt to stop upsetting thoughts, reduce anxiety, and/or increase a sense of safety, teens and others with OCD perform repetitive mental or physical acts, behaviors, or rituals, which are time-consuming and disrupt their lives. In many cases, these actions are irrational and have no logical connection to the feared obsession. For example, one teen with OCD reports that at one point in his life he felt compelled to jerk his head in each of the four directions to counteract obsessive thoughts that someone in his family was going to die. The teen knew that the action was senseless, but it lessened his fear. Such compulsive acts, as teen mental health expert Dr. Stan Kutcher explains, are "like having an itch on your arm and . . . scratching your leg instead."[10]

Other compulsions may be logically connected to the obsession but are more excessive than normal behavior. For example,

Excessive hand-washing is a common OCD-related compulsion. Individuals with OCD might engage in this behavior to ease their extreme and continuous distress about the possibility of being infected by harmful germs.

in an attempt to keep their belongings safe, healthy teens may double check their lockers before heading to class, or they may wash their hands after being around a sick friend. In contrast, teens with OCD are apt to become so obsessed with the thought that their locker is open that they check and recheck it dozens of times. Or, after being around someone who sneezes, teens with OCD may be so fearful that they have been contaminated that they shower for hours on end.

The relief these rituals offer is brief. Soon the obsession returns, which forces the teen to repeat the compulsive behavior. Moreover, as OCD symptoms worsen, obsessions recur more and more frequently, and sufferers wind up performing an increasing number and variety of rituals. As a result, OCD sufferers become caught in a seemingly endless loop that can take over their lives. As nineteen-year-old Clare explains,

> It began for me as lists. At any given time, I have 10 lists. I have a front page of the lists that I have in my list packet, and then I have the various lists. There are "To Do" lists, "To Study" lists, "Medicines to take," "When to take my medicines," etc. . . . Then I realized that I spell. I think of a conversation in my head and then realize that I had just spelled a word out while thinking. In conversations, I spell certain words and do not even realize it. Also, I have an 11 month old son and I color coordinate his bottles, and when his sitter messes up the rhythm, I have to empty and wash them all and begin the cycle of Red bottle, Green bottle, Purple bottle, etc . . . all over again. It seems stupid, but when I drive, I read every sign I see on the street, highway, freeway, or wherever. If I miss a sign, I get a feeling of panic, that I don't know something and now, I could be in danger, or be going the wrong way. I also have an obsession of order. Right now, I have a list in order of the obsessions I want to write about. Lastly, I count my bites, and when I walk upstairs, I count the stairs as well. These are all such minor, silly things . . . [but] my day cannot progress the way it should without these obsessions and compulsions of mine coming into play.[11]

To complicate matters, whereas children with OCD may not know that their actions are illogical, teens and adults with the disorder are usually aware that their obsessions and compulsive rituals make no sense, but they feel obliged to do them in order to gain relief. This distinguishes OCD from mental disorders like schizophrenia, in which individuals suffer from delusions and lose touch with reality. As author and OCD sufferer Jennifer Traig writes, "Obsessive-compulsives aren't delusional. OCD is not a psychosis. Sufferers never lose touch with reality. Sure, we do crazy things, but we know they're crazy. We don't want to do them at all, but we can't help ourselves. . . . I never thought it was a good idea to disinfect my binders, but I had to do it anyway."[12]

> "Obsessive-compulsives aren't delusional. OCD is not a psychosis. Sufferers never lose touch with reality."[12]
>
> —Jennifer Traig, OCD sufferer and author

Common Obsessions

In television and movies, people with OCD are usually depicted as being obsessed with cleanliness and order. Although these are common obsessions, they are not the only type. Obsessions take many forms. They tend to center around themes and can change over time. Moreover, individuals can have a variety of obsessions. One of the most common themes, especially among children and adolescents, is fear of contamination, which, depending on the person and their particular obsessions, can come from germs, bodily fluids, household and environmental chemicals, dirt, or food. Individuals with contamination obsessions fear they will contract an infection by touching or being near certain people or things that they believe might have been contaminated at some point. Josh, a young man who suffered with this type of obsession, recalls, "I viewed my school, and everything within it, as a microbial minefield, and the mere thought of bringing those filthy, disgusting books home and into my personal space made me physically ill."[13]

Contamination obsessions also often extend to fear of eating contaminated foods. As a result, individuals may limit what type

A healthy teen might double check the lock on his or her school locker before heading to class. A teen with OCD is likely to recheck the lock dozens of times out of fear that it will be left open and everything inside stolen.

of food they eat, and/or refuse to eat food touched by human hands. For example, at one point Ray St. John refused to eat anything that his mother touched.

Harming and Sexual Obsessions

Another obsessional theme that plagues many teens and others with OCD involves a fear of inadvertently causing harm to oneself or others. Individuals obsess about possible errors they might have made, such as leaving the stove turned on or unknowingly

Related Conditions

Two distinct mental disorders, trichotillomania and body dysmorphic disorder (BDD), are closely related to OCD. They produce OCD-like symptoms and, although they can affect people of all ages, are often found in adolescents. Individuals with trichotillomania compulsively pull out hair from their head, eyelashes, brows, and other parts of the body to relieve anxiety. This leaves them with embarrassing patches of missing hair, which they often go to great lengths to hide with hats and makeup. Trichotillomania is more prevalent in girls than boys.

BDD is prevalent in young teens who often feel self-conscious about their changing bodies. Sufferers have severe anxiety over real or imagined defects in their face or body. They perform repetitive acts such as picking at their skin, persistent mirror checking, and seeking reassurance to ease their anxiety, and they spend hours trying to conceal the perceived flaw with makeup and clothing. In many cases, the perceived flaw does not exist, and if it does, it is usually so minor that nobody but the sufferer notices it. Still, many teens with BDD refuse to take part in social activities or school functions in fear that their defect will be noticed.

hitting someone with their car. As a result, they check the stove or what they believe to be the accident site repeatedly because OCD makes them believe that they missed evidence of their mistake when they checked previously. For example, some OCD teen drivers report that they frequently circle a street dozens of times to make sure that they did not inadvertently run over a pedestrian.

Other harming obsessions, common to teens with OCD, involve the fear of causing intentional harm to others. These obsessions usually focus on violent urges and images. Although teens with OCD are no more likely to commit a violent act than anyone else, sufferers live in terror that they will actually act on these obsessions. At the same time, they feel ashamed for having such thoughts. This type of violent obsession frequently involves harming a parent, boyfriend, or girlfriend with a kitchen knife. Jared Douglas Kant, a young man who wrote a firsthand account of his teenage experience with OCD, compares such thoughts to "having a horror movie playing in your head that you can't turn off."[14]

Other violent obsessions that are prevalent in teens with OCD focus on sex. These often involve rape scenarios and first appear during puberty. Such obsessions are extremely disturbing and cause sufferers intense distress, guilt, and shame. As Kant recalls, "Just at the age when I was approaching my sexual awareness, I started having horrifying visions of myself committing sexual assaults on girls I found attractive. To me, rape is one of the worst things that a person can do to another human being, so I was extremely shaken by these thoughts."[15]

Religious Obsessions

Scrupulosity, the name given to hyper-religious obsessions, is another obsessional theme that plagues many teens with OCD. Scrupulosity is not the same as normal religious devotion. Teens and others with scrupulosity are plagued with persistent thoughts that they have offended God, even though there is no evidence to support their fears. To compensate, they spend hours praying and performing rituals. They often avoid certain foods, activities, clothing, and people that they fear are sinful. Traig suffered with scrupulosity as a teenager: "Sometimes I had to drop to my knees and pray in the middle of student council meeting and sometimes I had to hide under the bleachers and chant psalms."[16]

Perfection, Order, and Disorder

An urgent need for perfection, order, and/or symmetry is another common obsessional theme that affects many young people with OCD. Unlike healthy people who may be labeled as perfectionists because they always want to do their best, adolescents with this type of obsession fear that if things are imperfect, disordered, or asymmetrical something bad will happen to them or their loved ones or the sufferer will not be accepted by others. This type of obsession causes individuals to write and rewrite homework assignments, even at the expense of not getting the work completed; arrange and rearrange their possessions in a set order; and to do everything symmetrically. For instance, teens obsessed with symmetry may go out of their way when walking to class to make

15

an equal number of left and right turns or, if someone bumps their right side, they will purposefully bump into that person with their left side to make things even.

Whereas many adolescents with OCD are obsessed with order, others become hoarders because they have an intense fear of losing things that are somehow important to them or that they might need in the future. As a result, their rooms or homes overflow with useless items such as old broken toys, candy wrappers, clothes that no longer fit properly, old school papers, and more. In many cases, the accumulation fills up the entire living space. Some hoarders also amass an unhealthy number of animals. This obsession is more common in adults than in children and adolescents, but hoarding behavior often starts in the teen years. It is estimated that one in four people with OCD are hoarders; however, not all hoarders have OCD. Some have a distinct mental illness known as hoarding disorder.

Common Compulsions

Just as obsessions take many forms, so do compulsive behaviors, which are performed either mentally or physically as a coping method to lessen the fear and anxiety of obsessions. Whereas some compulsive acts, like praying to ease scrupulosity, connect logically to the obsession, others do not. Moreover, as OCD worsens, people frequently perform more and more-complex rituals that include multiple actions. For instance, Joe Wells, who at age sixteen wrote a book about his experiences with OCD, was obsessed with the thought that he was going to lose his soul. To protect himself, he performed a complex ritual that involved counting and tapping, which grew in length and complexity over time. He explains that he silently repeated

> I don't want to give my soul to anyone or anything as long as I tap this three times—"this" being any object near me. Three soon turned into five then ten then intricate sequences of numbers: "three, seven, five, three," "five, seven, five, ten, five, seven, five". . . This was not simple; I can tap at a speed of four taps a second but some of my sequences

were adding up to almost 100 taps: that's 25 seconds of tapping. This was hard to keep up, especially if I lost count and had to start again.[17]

Indeed, compulsive behaviors like Wells's that involve counting, tapping, repeating phrases in one's mind, or touching certain items in a specific but arbitrary way are quite common in teens with OCD. For example, to prevent her loved ones from being harmed, Nichole, a teenager with OCD, reports that she blinks two hundred times in a row counting by fives. Numbers also play a role in other compulsive behaviors. For illogical reasons, individuals often come up with lucky and unlucky numbers, which they believe can either save them from an obsessive thought or cause an obsession to come true. As a result, they will either go to extremes to avoid the unlucky number or to perform rituals involving the lucky number. Shayla, a young woman with OCD, comments,

> Three is my number. Everything must be done in threes or I fear that something bad will happen. Three touches to the doorknob, three checks to make sure my retainers are in the third drawer, three squeezes of shampoo, and so many more agonizing routines all done in threes. If I could turn my brain off to the threats my mind produces if things aren't done in threes, then my life wouldn't be one with OCD.[18]

Compulsive Washing and Checking Behaviors

Other compulsions linked to contamination obsessions involve washing. Individuals may wash their hands and shower so often that their skin becomes raw. They may also wash, rewash, and disinfect their possessions. St. John recalls, "I am astounded at the number of times I washed my homework because I felt it was contaminated. One would think that common sense and reason would have eventually stepped in and kept me from washing yet another piece of paper only to watch it disintegrate in water. But that is one of the hallmarks of OCD: The destruction of common sense."[19]

In addition to performing cleaning rituals, individuals obsessed with contamination frequently feel compelled to avoid specific objects, places, and people that they believe are contaminated. They report avoiding walking past hospitals, refusing to go to public places, refusing to sit on certain pieces of furniture, or refusing to come in contact with certain people. In severe cases, teens with this problem refuse to go to school.

Checking and rechecking is another type of compulsive behavior. Checking behavior can be so repetitive that it can keep individuals from getting anything done. For example, students with this compulsive behavior may spend so much time checking the heading on a standardized test that they never get to answer the questions.

Another type of checking compulsion involves repeatedly seeking reassurance. It is a common compulsive behavior among children and teens with OCD. Individuals with this compulsion repeatedly ask others questions related to their obsessions in hopes that the answer will ease their anxiety. As an article on the website of the OCD Center of Los Angeles explains,

> "People with Obsessive Compulsive Disorder (OCD) who experience the pain and terror brought on by unwanted intrusive thoughts will use whatever means necessary to alleviate their discomfort."[20]
>
> —OCD Center of Los Angeles

People with Obsessive Compulsive Disorder (OCD) who experience the pain and terror brought on by unwanted intrusive thoughts will use whatever means necessary to alleviate their discomfort. If they can't make themselves feel sure about something internally, they reach out to the nearest person who they think can do it for them. . . . For example, a person with OCD may compulsively ask friends and family if they have washed their hands enough, or if they have run someone over with the car.[20]

OCD Afflicts 2.2 Million Americans

Obsessive-compulsive disorder, more commonly known as OCD, is not the most common anxiety disorder (as can be seen in this graph). However, unlike some other disorders, OCD often develops during childhood or adolescence. In fact, one-quarter of all cases begin by age fourteen. Boys are more likely to develop the disorder during childhood, and girls are more likely to develop it in their teens to early twenties.

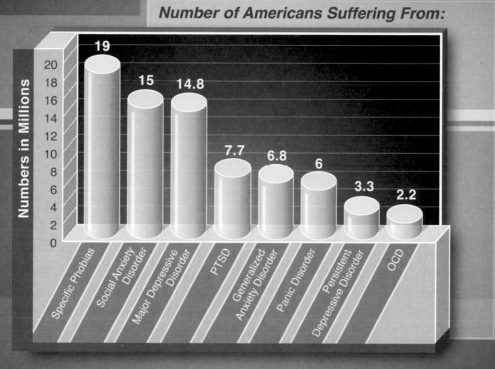

Number of Americans Suffering From:

Source: Anxiety and Depression Association of America, "Facts and Statistics," September 2014. www.adaa.org.

Who Gets OCD?

According to the National Institute of Mental Health, 2.2 million Americans have OCD. Some estimates are higher, however, because many OCD sufferers—especially children and teens with the condition—go undiagnosed. Beyond OCD, an organization dedicated to helping people with OCD, reports that the disorder affects one in forty American adults and one in one hundred

The Difference Between Perfectionism and OCD

Many individuals with OCD appear to be perfectionists. However, there is a difference between being a perfectionist and needing to do things perfectly due to OCD. In *The OCD Answer Book*, psychologist Patrick B. McGrath explains,

If you can do things without spending hours and hours on little details for ordinary tasks, this is not OCD. If you have a hobby and you spend hours on something related to the hobby, that is not OCD either. But if you spend hours on everyday tasks because you would be too anxious to have them not be perfect, then that could be OCD. Or, if you have a hobby, but you never actually complete anything because you can never get it to be "just right," then that could be OCD as well. For perfectionism to meet the criteria for OCD, you would probably have obsessive thoughts telling you that you had to do things perfectly—most likely that you would not be accepted by others if you were not perfect. You would need to perform compulsive behaviors to get things done perfectly, even at the expense of getting those things done on time or even at the expense of your relationships with others.

Patrick B. McGrath, *The OCD Answer Book*. Naperville, IL: Sourcebooks, 2007, p. 30.

American children and teens. In addition, the disorder is equally common among males and females.

OCD is not limited to Americans. People of all ethnicities, socioeconomic levels, and cultures are affected. In fact, the World Health Organization ranks OCD as one of the top twenty causes of illness-related disability in the world in people ages fifteen to forty-four.

OCD often begins in childhood or during adolescence. Although people can develop OCD at any age, most cases develop by age twenty-five. According to the Anxiety and Depression Association of America, one-quarter of all cases begin by age fourteen. Boys are more likely to develop the disorder during child-hood, and girls are more likely to develop it in their teens to early twenties. When OCD begins in childhood, it is known as early-onset OCD. When it begins at a later time, it is known as late-onset OCD.

Some people with OCD also have other mental disorders. Among these are general anxiety disorders, depression, eating disorders, Tourette's syndrome, autism, attention-deficit/hyper-activity disorder, and bipolar disease. These conditions can com-plicate OCD cases but are usually separate from OCD.

Clearly, no matter who gets OCD, the condition causes indi-viduals great distress. OCD is a serious anxiety disorder, not to be confused with quirky behavior, normal worries, habits, or silly superstitions. Teens and others with OCD do not want to have distressing obsessions, nor do they want to perform compulsive acts. They usually know that their thoughts and rituals are irratio-nal, but once they get caught in an obsessive-compulsive cycle, they find it difficult to stop.

CHAPTER TWO

What Causes OCD?

Scientists have not discovered a single proven cause of OCD. Research points to a number of possible risk factors that may predispose teens and others to developing the condition. These include unusual brain activity, problems related to brain chemistry, genetics, a bacterial infection, and environmental factors.

Unusual Brain Activity

In an attempt to learn more about OCD, scientists have conducted a number of studies in which they have used imaging devices such as magnetic resonance imaging and positron emission tomography to study the brains of subjects with OCD. The results indicate that there are differences in brain activity in certain areas of the brains of patients with OCD when compared to those of people without the ailment. Scientists theorize that there is a link between these abnormalities and the development of OCD.

Three areas of the brain—the orbital frontal cortex, the caudate nucleus, and the cingulate gyrus—appear to be overactive in people with OCD. The first of these brain structures, the orbital frontal cortex, is part of the frontal lobe that is located in the cerebrum. The orbital frontal cortex is involved in controlling thinking and reasoning, weighing outcomes, and regulating behavior. Scientists theorize that overactivity in the orbital frontal cortex may cause individuals to make bad judgments and come up with illogical plans that reinforce the idea that performing rituals will protect them from harm and ease obsessions.

Moreover, the orbital frontal cortex and other areas of the cerebrum are not fully developed in teens. This puts all adolescents at a disadvantage concerning judgment, decision making, and assessing the effects of their behavior. As a result, teens with OCD may believe more strongly than adults that a compulsive behavior is the correct response to unsettling thoughts. Complicating matters further, a part of the cerebrum that controls feelings of pleasure, motivation, and addiction seems to be overdeveloped in teenagers compared to children and adults. So, when a teen performs a ritual in an effort to ease an obsession, the ritual is apt to provide the teen with more relief than it would a child or adult, thus making it more likely that the teen will continue the behavior.

Imaging tests have also found that another part of the brain, the caudate nucleus, is overactive in people with OCD. The caudate nucleus is located near the center of the cerebrum in a part of the brain known as the basal ganglia. It is responsible for controlling repetitive behaviors and filtering out unimportant or unnecessary information. It also serves as a relay station for information going back and forth between various areas of the brain. Scientists hypothesize that hyperactivity in the caudate nucleus compromises its ability to screen out irrelevant information. So, instead of filtering out unnecessary information, it sends the information on to other parts of the brain that act on it. This may be why people with OCD cannot let go of obsessive thoughts. In addition, hyperactivity in this part of the brain, which is linked to controlling movement, may be responsible for triggering repetitive rituals involving movements like cleaning and checking.

The cingulate gyrus is also linked to OCD. It is located in the cerebrum and is a part of a network of nerves known as the brain's limbic system. It is involved in emotional responses. It regulates a person's response to aggression and manages feelings of fear and dread. When it is overactive, it is believed to contribute to the intense feelings of fear caused by obsessive thoughts and to directing individuals to perform compulsive acts as a response to fear.

Interestingly, a circuit, which imaging tests suggest is also overactive, connects these three areas of the brain. It is possible that overactivity within this circuit makes it difficult for the brain

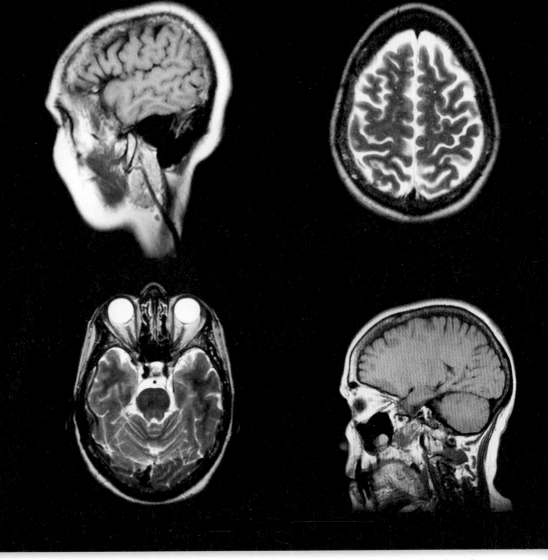

Doctors and medical researchers can see inside the brain using various imaging techniques including magnetic resonance imaging, or MRI (shown). Imaging of this sort reveals differences in brain activity in people with and without OCD.

to turn off obsessive thoughts and accompanying compulsive behaviors. An article on the OCD-UK website explains that

when this circuit is activated . . . impulses are brought to your attention and cause you to perform a particular behavior that appropriately addresses the impulse. For example, after a visit to the bathroom, you may begin to wash your hands to remove any harmful germs you may have encountered. Once you have performed the appropriate behavior . . . the impulse from this brain circuit diminishes and you stop washing your hands and go about your day. It has been suggested that if you have OCD, your brain has difficulty turning off or ignoring impulses from this circuit. This, in turn means the obsessions and compulsions continue leading you to wash your hands again and again.[21]

A Chemical Imbalance

Abnormalities in brain chemistry also seem to play a part in causing OCD. A 2016 University of Minnesota study that compared brain scans of teenagers with OCD to those of healthy teenagers found that the connections between neurons in the brains of teens with OCD were weaker than in the brains of healthy teens. Scientists speculate that this lower connectivity is linked to a deficiency in the production and flow of the neurotransmitter serotonin.

Neurotransmitters are chemicals that relay messages between neurons, or brain cells. There are at least fifty different types of neurotransmitters. Each carries different types of messages to different areas of the brain. Serotonin carries messages related to behavior and mood between the orbital frontal cortex and the basal ganglia. High levels of serotonin are associated with feelings of general well-being. In contrast, a serotonin deficiency is associated with anxiety, edginess, lack of mental clarity, and negative thoughts and feelings—emotions and behaviors that also play a role in OCD.

Scientists theorize that a problem with the production and flow of serotonin heightens feelings of anxiety in people with OCD, causing their brains to overreact to distressing thoughts. As an article on the KidsHealth website explains, "When the flow of serotonin is blocked [reduced], the brain's 'alarm system' overreacts and misinterprets information. 'False alarms' mistakenly trigger danger messages. Instead of the brain filtering out these unnecessary thoughts, the mind dwells on them—and the person experiences unrealistic fear and doubt."[22]

Making matters worse for teenagers, due to differences in brain development, serotonin levels are normally at their lowest levels for all individuals during the teen years. Therefore, the deficiency is especially severe in teens with OCD, which may be one reason why OCD often begins during adolescence.

OCD Runs in Families

Genetic factors appear to be another component in predisposing people to developing OCD. Fifteen studies over the last twenty years indicate that OCD runs in families, and a person's risk of developing the disorder is higher if one's parents or siblings have the disorder. Although the risk ratio varies depending on the particular study, research results suggest that as many as 37 percent of individuals with OCD have a parent with the disorder, and as many as 21 percent have a sibling with the disorder. Research has also shown that there is an inverse relationship between the age of onset of OCD and a person's potential risk of developing the disorder. Transmission of OCD appears to occur anywhere from 13 to 32 percent more often if an individual's parent developed OCD by age seventeen as compared to individuals whose parents developed OCD after age seventeen. Scientists do not know why this is so.

"When the flow of serotonin is blocked [reduced], the brain's 'alarm system' overreacts and misinterprets information. 'False alarms' mistakenly trigger danger messages. Instead of the brain filtering out these unnecessary thoughts, the mind dwells on them—and the person experiences unrealistic fear and doubt."[22]

—KidsHealth, a website that provides information on health issues for young people

Studies of pairs of twins further support a familial link in predisposing individuals to OCD. The studies found that in 80 to 87

The Teen Brain

The brains of teenagers are still developing. In hopes of learning what causes mental illnesses, and why many mental illnesses begin during adolescence, scientists have been studying the differences between teen and adult brains. One difference they have found is that the areas of an adolescent's brain responsible for controlling impulses and planning ahead are not fully developed. Another difference is that changes in brain circuitry during adolescence appear to intensify a teenager's emotional reactions to different experiences. Other differences involve how teens use the brain. The brain is at its peak for learning during the teen years. However, brain imaging and behavioral tests suggest that, when performing similar tasks involving impulse control or in reaction to emotional subject matter, adolescents and adults use different parts of the brain.

Scientists are continuing to study the teen brain. But they have drawn some conclusions from what they have learned. An article on the NIMH web site explains: "One interpretation of all these findings is that in teens, the parts of the brain involved in emotional responses are fully online, or even more active than in adults, while the parts of the brain involved in keeping emotional, impulsive responses in check are still reaching maturity."

National Institute of Mental Health, "The Teen Brain Still Under Construction," 2011. www.nimh.nih.gov.

percent of cases in which one identical twin has OCD, the other twin also has the condition. In comparison, in 47 to 50 percent of cases in which one fraternal twin has OCD, the other twin also has it. Because identical twins have identical genes but fraternal twins do not, these findings support the theory that genetics is involved in the development of OCD, but it is not the sole cause of the condition. If the cause of OCD was purely genetic, pairs of identical twins would both have the condition or both not have it.

Links to Mutant Genes

Even if genetics is not the sole cause of OCD, there is enough evidence to conclude that genes play a key role in increasing a person's risk of developing the disorder. Therefore, scientists have been investigating whether teens and others with OCD share a specific gene or group of genes that puts them at risk of developing OCD. In research conducted at seven universities and published in 2014, scientists scanned the genomes of fourteen hundred people with OCD and compared the scans to those of a control group. The scientists looked for a correlation between OCD and genetic markers. Genetic markers are not specific abnormalities but rather are indicators that an abnormal gene is located nearby.

Researchers found that the subjects with OCD were more likely to have a genetic marker located near a gene called PTPRD than those in the control group. The gene is involved in learning and memory. Whether a variant of PTPRD is involved in causing OCD requires further study. As study leader Gerald Nestadt of Johns Hopkins University School of Medicine explains, "If this finding is confirmed, it could be useful. . . . OCD research has lagged behind other psychiatric disorders in terms of genetics. We hope this interesting finding brings us closer to making better sense of it—and helps us find ways to treat it."[23]

> "OCD research has lagged behind other psychiatric disorders in terms of genetics."[23]
>
> —Gerald Nestadt, director of the Obsessive-Compulsive Disorder Program at Johns Hopkins School of Medicine

Other researchers have focused on investigating genes that are involved in the production and transportation of serotonin. In a 2008 National Institute of Mental Health (NIMH) study, researchers looked at a gene known as SLC6A4, which is responsible for the movement of serotonin between neurons. In this study scientists compared the gene in 295 people with OCD and 657 people without OCD. They found two abnormalities in the gene in 9.3 percent of the people with OCD, compared to the abnormalities being present in only 5.9 percent of the people who did not have OCD.

Since flaws in serotonin production and transmission are associated with OCD, the researchers were not surprised by their discoveries. However, the involvement of another gene, known as SLITRK5, surprised researchers at Weill Cornell Medical College. SLITRK5 is a gene found in cells related to the circulatory system. In 2010, in an effort to better understand the role SLITRK5 plays in the blood system, researchers disabled the gene in laboratory mice. The researchers were surprised to find that the genetically altered mice exhibited OCD-like symptoms that included undue anxiety and excessive grooming behavior.

Based on this discovery, the researchers investigated the animals' brain functions. They found structural abnormalities in the area of the brain that houses the caudate nucleus. Specifically, nerve cells in this section of the brain were less complex than in the brains of mice in the control group. Interestingly, these nerve cells are involved in transmitting and receiving information from the frontal cortex. The researchers do not know whether a mutation of the SLITRK5 gene has a similar effect on humans without conducting further studies. However, the data suggests that SLITRK5 may play a key part in the development of OCD. "We can't draw direct parallels between mice and humans, because OCD behavior in mice shows up as excessive self-grooming, and in humans there is a broad spectrum of behaviors, from hand-washing to other compulsive actions as well as obsessive thoughts," says Dr. Francis S.Y. Lee, the study's senior coinvestigator. "But our finding of altered brain functioning suggests a very strong link at this point to some of the issues seen in humans."[24]

Bacterial Infections

Although genetic factors appear to play an important role in determining who develops OCD, OCD is a complex condition that seems to have multiple causes. Another possible cause of some cases of OCD is related to streptococcus bacteria. It causes illnesses like scarlet fever and strep throat. According to studies conducted by the NIMH, some children and adolescents, ages three through fourteen, develop pediatric autoimmune neuropsychiatric disorders associated with streptococcal infections (PANDAS) after a bout of strep throat. PANDAS is characterized by the sudden onset of severe obsessions and compulsive behaviors often accompanied by physical tics (involuntary movements), anxiety, sleep disturbances, uncontrolled emotions, and irritability. According to the NIMH, "The symptoms are usually dramatic, happen 'overnight and out of the blue,' and can include motor and/or vocal tics, obsessions, and/or compulsions."[25] In contrast, most cases of OCD unrelated to PANDAS usually develop and worsen gradually.

Another difference is that unlike most cases of OCD, PANDAS-related OCD is episodic. Over time, OCD symptoms often disappear in young people suffering from PANDAS only to return with greater intensity if the patient contracts another strep infection. As the NIMH explains,

> Patients with PANDAS have a very sudden onset or worsening of their symptoms, followed by a slow, gradual improvement. If they get another strep infection, their symptoms suddenly worsen again. The increased symptom severity usually persists for at least several weeks, but may last for several months or longer . . . then seem to gradually fade away, and the children often enjoy a few weeks or several months without problems. When they have another strep throat infection . . . OCD [symptoms] may return just as suddenly and dramatically as they did previously.[26]

Scientists think that PANDAS occurs when antibodies produced by the immune system to fight the streptococcus bacteria mistake healthy tissue in the basal ganglia for strep bacteria. As a result, the antibodies attack the healthy brain tissue, triggering OCD symptoms. This is known as an autoimmune response. Researchers speculate that infections caused by the flu virus, Lyme disease, and mononucleosis may also cause OCD symptoms in susceptible young people. As yet, this theory has not been proved, but future research may validate it.

Most children and adolescents who contract a strep or other infection do not get PANDAS. However, when young children contract PANDAS, the change in their behavior is sudden and obvious, making it easy for parents to determine that something is wrong. According to the International OCD Foundation, "When you meet a parent of a child with PANDAS . . . you will hear the same panicked story over and over. A child who was happy at

A Vicious Cycle

People with OCD get caught in a vicious cycle. They experience distressing and repetitive thoughts, or obsessions, which cause them intense anxiety. In an effort to ease their anxiety, they perform rituals, or compulsive behaviors. The compulsion provides them with temporary relief. The obsession recurs and the cycle is repeated over and over again.

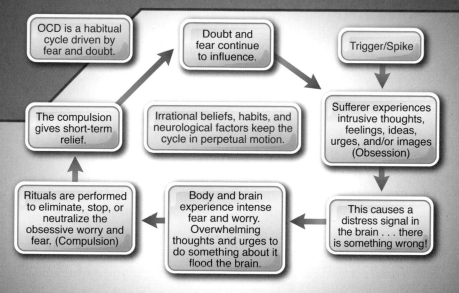

OCD is a habitual cycle driven by fear and doubt.

Doubt and fear continue to influence.

Trigger/Spike

The compulsion gives short-term relief.

Irrational beliefs, habits, and neurological factors keep the cycle in perpetual motion.

Sufferer experiences intrusive thoughts, feelings, ideas, urges, and/or images (Obsession)

Rituals are performed to eliminate, stop, or neutralize the obsessive worry and fear. (Compulsion)

Body and brain experience intense fear and worry. Overwhelming thoughts and urges to do something about it flood the brain.

This causes a distress signal in the brain . . . there is something wrong!

Source: The OCD Therapy Clinic, "What Is OCD?," 2016. www.helpforocd.co.uk.

home and at school and was social and athletic is now walking in circles for hours, washing hands until they bleed, asking the same questions over and over and over. . . . These parents will tell you in detail about the day that their child changed."[27]

In contrast, when tweens and young teens contract PANDAS, it is often difficult for parents to recognize that something is wrong. In many cases, tweens and young teens may already be acting emotional and anxious due to hormonal changes related to the onset of puberty, which makes the reason for the change in their behavior less obvious. Moreover, due to unwarranted feelings of shame or guilt, tweens and teens are more likely to hide PANDAS symptoms from their family than young children are.

Other Possible Factors

OCD is a puzzling condition. There appears to be a number of possible causes. The general consensus is that genetic and biological makeup predisposes teens and others to developing the disorder, and environmental factors often trigger or quicken its onset. In fact, a number of studies suggest that there is a connection between traumatic life events and OCD.

It is normal for frightening or painful events to cause victims anxiety, worry, and fear and for a person's behavior to change in response to a traumatic experience. In susceptible individuals, these factors seem to trigger the onset of OCD. In fact, a University of California, Los Angeles study found that 30 percent of people with OCD have been victims of physical, sexual, or psychological trauma.

Moreover, among patients with OCD, those who had experienced one or more traumatic life events were found to have more severe cases of OCD than were other patients. A study conducted by the NIMH found that among 265 patients admitted to the NIMH's OCD clinic, the severity of the subjects' symptoms correlated with a history of trauma. Similarly, an investigation of 104 patients admitted to McLean Hospital's OCD Institute for severe OCD found that 82 percent of the patients reported a history of trauma.

"Our findings are important because they might explain why . . . anxiety disorders [including OCD] seem to spike during adolescence or just before adolescence."[28]

—Dr. Siobhan S. Pattwell, a postdoctoral fellow at the Sackler Institute for Developmental Psychobiology at Weill Cornell Medical School

Complicating matters for teens, research suggests that due to the developmental differences in the adolescent brain, teenagers react to trauma longer and more intensely than adults and children do. A 2012 Weill Cornell Medical School study found that when an adolescent's brain perceives a threat, his or her emotional reaction to the threat remains high even after the threat is reduced, which makes it difficult for teens, in general, and teens with OCD, in particular, to overcome fears. This may

32

OCD and Neurotransmitters

Serotonin is just one of many neurotransmitters that allow the different parts of the brain to communicate with each other. Researchers are investigating what, if any, role other neurotransmitters play in the development and maintenance of OCD. Dopamine is one of these neurotransmitters. It helps regulate mood and controls impulses and emotional responses. It is essential to movement control and is involved in the pleasure-reward area of the brain. Studies suggest that people with OCD have higher-than-normal levels of dopamine. Researchers theorize that overproduction of dopamine is linked to OCD. More research is needed to find out what this link may be.

Another neurotransmitter, glutamate, is also being investigated. Glutamate is the most abundant neurotransmitter in the brain. It is critical to neurons communicating with each other in every part of the brain. It also helps regulate brain functions related to thought, memory, and learning. A number of studies have detected higher-than-normal levels of glutamate in the brains of people with OCD. Scientists theorize that abnormally high levels of glutamate can damage neurons, which would impair communication between the different areas of the brain. This, in turn, could produce behaviors related to OCD.

explain why adults are usually better able to deal with and move on from fear-inducing events than are teenagers. It may also explain why OCD often begins in the teen years. As the study's lead author, Dr. Siobhan S. Pattwell, explains, "Our findings are important because they might explain why . . . anxiety disorders [including OCD] seem to spike during adolescence or just before adolescence."[28]

Adding to the problem is the fact that heightened emotions caused by hormonal changes can make seemingly minor events distressing to teens. The combination of differences in the adolescent brain, which make it difficult for teens to overcome fear, and hormonal factors that cause heightened emotional responses, may explain why events that might not affect others may trigger OCD symptoms in teens that are already at risk of developing the disorder. Such events include, but are not limited to, being involved in an accident, changing schools, or starting college.

Dan, a young man who developed OCD as an adolescent, experienced this type of event shortly before he exhibited symptoms of the disorder. Dan was tossing the mouthpiece of a clarinet in the air when it accidentally hit his friend in the eye. Although his friend's injury was not severe, it required several stitches. Dan became traumatized about what had happened. He became obsessed by the thought that he would inadvertently harm his loved ones and began performing rituals to protect them. Although it is not likely that this event caused Dan to get OCD—he was already susceptible to the disorder—it may have triggered the onset of OCD symptoms. In her blog, Dan's mother, Janet Singer, explains, "I know that this incident didn't cause Dan's OCD, and that it was bound to appear sooner or later. But maybe this event made it sooner. Perhaps it was like The Perfect Storm . . . everything was in the right place at the right time to kick start the OCD."[29]

Clearly, there appear to be multiple causes of OCD. A combination of genetics, structural brain abnormalities, brain chemistry, and environmental factors all seem to play a role. It is possible that future research may pinpoint an exact cause, which may eventually lead to the development of a cure. Until that time, individuals with OCD must face the challenge of living with the disorder.

CHAPTER THREE

What Is It Like to Live with OCD?

Teens and others with OCD face many challenges. Obsessive thoughts and time-consuming rituals can cause problems in almost every aspect of a person's life. As Shayla, a teen with OCD, explains,

> Whether it's a walk to class or a bedtime routine, OCD takes over every simple task I try to perform. . . . I have tried for years and years to ignore my disorder and just know that the sun will rise whether I touch the door in specific places as I close it behind or not, but that can't stop me from continuing my routines. . . . Living with OCD is not something I am particularly fond of, but it is something I have learned to deal with. Life would be more free [without OCD].[30]

Problems at Home

Home and family life can be trying for people with OCD and their families. This is especially true for teens, who are at a time of transition in their lives and often find themselves at odds with their parents. According to teen mental health expert Dr. Stan Kutcher, "Adolescence is the time when people start to consolidate their identity and experiment with independence; two things that can cause a lot of conflict with their families."[31]

OCD adds to the normal challenges of adolescence and often leads to misunderstandings between young people and their families. Teens with OCD are often ashamed of their thoughts and rituals and, therefore, try to keep their symptoms secret. As a result, family members may think that teens with contamination obsessions, for example, are being rebellious when they monopolize the bathroom for hours or refuse to do chores like taking out the trash or clearing the table. This type of misunderstanding can be frustrating for everyone and can lead to anger and heated arguments.

In other cases, even when family members know that a teen has OCD, they may not understand what it is like to have the disorder and may think they are being helpful by advising teens to just stop thinking unpleasant thoughts and performing compulsive acts. Although well meaning, this type of advice makes teens with OCD feel more anxious and out of control. As Emily, a college student with OCD, explains, "Things such as 'Just stop, Emily!' 'Calm down,' 'It's all in your head'. . . would be said to me on an everyday basis by family, friends, peers, and teachers, which sent me further down the spiral and into a depressed state."[32]

> "OCD can dominate family life, straining relationships.
> Perhaps in no other psychological disorder is the family so inexorably brought into the patient's illness than OCD."[34]
>
> —Barbara Van Noppen, a psychologist and the codirector of the Keck School of Medicine OCD Treatment and Research Program in Los Angeles

Even if family members understand that teens with OCD cannot control their symptoms, the condition puts a strain on everyone and often disrupts normal family life. "OCD can touch virtually every facet of day-to-day life," says Jared Douglas Kant, a young man who developed OCD as a child. "When one family member spends hours locked in the bathroom washing, goes through elaborate rituals before meals, or becomes very upset when personal possessions are moved even slightly, it affects the quality of life of the family as well."[33]

At the same time, OCD sufferers struggle with feelings of guilt brought about by the toll the disorder takes on their family. Yet there is little teens and others with OCD can do to make things right. "OCD can dominate family life, straining relationships," says OCD therapist Barbara Van Noppen. "Perhaps in no other psychological disorder is the family so inexorably brought into the patient's illness than OCD."[34]

Common Obsessions and Compulsions of OCD

OCD is characterized by a variety of obsessions and compulsions. Although these may vary, medical experts have identified some of the most common obsessions and compulsions.

Obsessions	Compulsions
Common obsessions include:	**Common compulsions include:**
Fear of dirt or contamination by germs	Repeatedly bathing, showering, or washing hands
	Refusing to shake hands or touch doorknobs
Fear of causing harm to another	Repeatedly checking things, such as locks or stoves
Fear of making a mistake	Constantly counting, mentally or aloud, while performing routine tasks
Fear of being embarrassed or behaving in a socially unacceptable manner	Constantly arranging things in a certain way
	Eating foods in a specific order
Fear of thinking sinful thoughts	Being stuck on words, images, or thoughts, usually disturbing, that won't go away and can interfere with sleep
Need for order, symmetry, or exactness	Repeating specific words, phrases, or prayers
Excessive doubt and the need for constant reassurance	Needing to perform tasks a certain number of times
	Collecting or hoarding items with no apparent value

Source: WebMD, "Obsessive-Compulsive Disorder." www.webmd.com.

As a matter of fact, sometimes family members can become too involved. Problems arise for teens with OCD when well-meaning family members unintentionally enable OCD behaviors by adapting to and helping teens with their rituals. When family members do things like offering teens with OCD repeated reassurance or providing them with unlimited cleaning supplies, rather than helping, these actions reinforce the teen's compulsive behaviors. So do other enabling actions, such as rearranging things in the house to meet the teen's obsession with symmetry, washing and rewashing clothes, assisting in checking behaviors, or changing family plans

OCD and Substance Abuse

In an attempt to get relief from obsessions and compulsive behaviors, many teens with OCD self-medicate by abusing alcohol or drugs. Although these substances may offer temporary relief from anxiety, over time they can exacerbate OCD symptoms and problems associated with the disorder. Substance abuse also negatively impacts a person's physical health, sleep, eating habits, and learning ability. It can cause financial, legal, and health problems. And it also can lead to addiction.

Teens with OCD are vulnerable to addiction. The compulsive nature of the disorder makes it difficult for them to stop behavior that leads to drug or alcohol addiction. As an article on DualDiagnosis.org explains, "Addiction itself is a compulsive condition, causing the repetitive pursuit of a destructive substance or behavior in spite of the negative consequences." In fact, research suggests that substance abuse disorders are found in about 25 percent of the people who seek treatment for OCD. Moreover, just as many teens keep their disorder secret, they are also secretive about their substance abuse. Therefore, substance abuse problems may be advanced before teens with OCD seek help.

DualDiagnosis.org, "Obsessive Compulsive Disorder and Addiction." www.dualdiagnosis.org.

to accommodate the teen's strict routines and rituals. According to child and adolescent psychiatrist Gail Bernstein,

> Most parents who have a child with OCD "accommodate" to their child's OCD symptoms. This means that they change family routines or interactions with their child in a way that allows the child to engage in the OCD rituals and they may participate in rituals with their child. Although this may seem to be supportive to the children, it is counterproductive in that it allows the children with OCD to continue engaging in their impairing OCD symptoms.[35]

Difficulties at School and Work

Other challenges arise outside the home for teens with OCD. The condition can cause problems for young people at school and at work. Indeed, having OCD can negatively affect a student's academic performance. Paying attention in class can be difficult when obsessive thoughts fill the mind, mental compulsions can keep students off task, and physical compulsions like checking and washing rituals can make students be late for or miss classes. Fear of germs can make it almost impossible for students to participate in science labs or touch items like doorknobs, classroom furniture, lockers, or library books, for example. Ray St. John recalls,

> For me, OCD stood in front of a lot of possible school progress that I could have made. I actually used homework papers or pages from textbooks as barriers to use to open doors with and touch things that I didn't want to touch. For example, I didn't study for my ACT standardized test because I had used a portion of the study book to touch things, such as door handles that I was convinced had been contaminated.[36]

Other problems arise due to obsessive perfectionism and fear of making mistakes. These issues can cause young people to erase, redo, and check their work so many times that they fail to complete their assignments. As a result, their grades fall. Moreover, since many teens with OCD do not tell their teachers about their condition, teachers may not understand what the problem is and think that the student is being irresponsible, uninterested, or lazy. As St. John explains,

> Many times I heard my parents and teachers say things like: . . . Why is it that you always need extra homework sheets? Why should I let you turn your homework in late again? Why didn't you hear me the first two times I told the class about the assignment? . . . Looking back, I wished I had words to explain what OCD was doing to me. I wanted to let others know that I wasn't being rude, belligerent, or purposefully trying to get away with something. It was just that my obsessions were often churning so fast in my brain that it was hard for any new information to break through.[37]

As part of a science class, high school students dissect a frog. A student with OCD who is terrified of germs would have great difficulty carrying out this type of assignment.

The same issues can cause similar problems for OCD sufferers at work, making it difficult for teens with OCD to hold down a job.

Making Friends

OCD can also affect a sufferer's social life. Young people with OCD often find it difficult to make—and keep—friends. Their recurring, distressing thoughts and compulsive rituals can take up so much of their time that they do not have time to connect with others or to participate in activities that might help them make friends. Additionally, their compulsive behaviors can make teens with OCD appear strange or crazy to other teens who may not understand why teens with OCD act the way they do and, therefore, avoid them. Indeed, children and teens with OCD are frequently teased or bullied because of their odd behavior. Even if they are not ridiculed, they often find it difficult to fit in. Jennifer Traig recalls her high school years: "I had no peers. What teenager spends her free time reading psalms and sterilizing salad tongs? These are activities you do alone. There are no washing societies."[38]

In other cases, teens with OCD purposely isolate themselves in an attempt to keep their condition secret or as a way to deal with their obsessions and compulsive behaviors. It is not uncommon for individuals with OCD to refuse to be around certain people, including close friends, due to contamination, harming, or religious obsessions. Joe Wells writes of his early teens, "I did not have that many friends. . . . It was not because people did not like me, but that I did not want to go round to friends' houses or down [to] the park because I thought it was likely that I would either be seen protecting myself from poison or I would potentially become contaminated with poison."[39]

> "I did not have that many friends. . . . It was not because people did not like me, but that I did not want to go round to friends' houses or down [to] the park because I thought it was likely that I would either be seen protecting myself from poison or I would potentially become contaminated with poison."[39]
>
> —Joe Wells, who developed OCD as a child and later wrote a book about his experiences with the disorder

Emotional Issues

The challenges of living with OCD can lead to emotional problems. When combined with shifting hormonal levels and the stress of establishing independence, such problems can have a profound effect on adolescents. For instance, feelings of guilt and shame in response to harming and sexual obsessions can be especially intense among adolescents. They may come to think of themselves as depraved, evil people when, in reality, they are not. "OCD is not a personality trait, not even a personality disorder. . . . There is nothing to be ashamed of or feel embarrassed about. . . . Our symptoms do not define our identity,"[40] explains Argentinian singer and OCD sufferer Romina Vitale. However, it can be difficult for teens with OCD to separate their symptoms from their sense of self. As a result, their confidence and self-esteem plummet. Low self-confidence and low self-esteem can negatively affect a person's social life as well as his or her school and work performance.

> "OCD is not a personality trait, not even a personality disorder. . . . There is nothing to be ashamed of or feel embarrassed about. . . . Our symptoms do not define our identity."[40]
>
> —Romina Vitale, a popular Argentinian singer and OCD awareness advocate

Depression is another emotional issue many teens with OCD face. About 62 percent of teens with OCD struggle with depression. As life-long OCD sufferer Jill Armstrong explains,

Much of my childhood and younger adult years were taken from me by OCD. . . . I rarely let anyone see my anguish and hid my rituals to protect myself from the scrutiny and misunderstanding from others. I had developed an unbelievable amount of shame over the years, combined with low self-esteem. If I couldn't stand up to a voice in my head, how could I stand up to others? I managed to push my way through life staggering between my okay times and lows but . . . the lows started to increase and with more severity.[41]

Depression is a serious problem. It is a mental disorder characterized by long-lasting, strong feelings of despair. At its worst, it can cause people to feel so hopeless that they commit suicide. Research suggests that 5 to 25 percent of people with OCD have

Signs of Suicidal Behavior

Some teens with OCD become so depressed that they commit suicide or attempt to do so. Research suggests that there are certain warning signs that indicate a person is suffering from depression and that precede most teen suicides. In most cases, not all of these signs are present. But it is important to know what they are. According to Teen Suicide, a website dedicated to teen suicide prevention, warning signs include the following:

- Disinterest in favorite extracurricular activities
- Problems at work and losing interest in a job
- Substance abuse, including alcohol and drug (illegal and legal drugs) use
- Behavioral problems
- Withdrawing from family and friends
- Sleep changes
- Changes in eating habits
- Begins to neglect hygiene and other matters of personal appearance
- Emotional distress brings on physical complaints (aches, fatigues, migraines)
- Hard time concentrating and paying attention
- Declining grades in school
- Loss of interest in schoolwork
- Risk-taking behaviors
- Complains more frequently of boredom
- Does not respond as before to praise

Teen Suicide, "Teen Suicide Warning Signs." www.teensuicide.us.

attempted suicide at some point in their lives, and many others have contemplated taking their own lives. OCD sufferer Alison Dotson was one of these individuals. "I actually had considered suicide," she confesses. "I had become so distraught that there were moments when I truly felt death was the only escape. . . . I did want to live, but only if my life didn't have to continue as it had been going."[42]

Many young people with OCD are teased or bullied and keep to themselves. Some choose to stay away from their peers because they fear contamination or that harm will come to themselves or to others.

Secondary Physical Issues

In addition to causing emotional and social problems, OCD can negatively impact a person's physical health. Excessive washing, for instance, causes chapped and bleeding skin, along with open sores and blisters. Ironically, having open sores and blisters makes individuals vulnerable to the very germs they are trying to eliminate. According to medical writer Ross Bonander, "Our skin can be regarded as the first line of defense against pathogens getting into our bodies, so the last thing you want to do is to reduce the efficacy of that blockade by creating open sores such as blisters."[43] Making matters worse, many teens also have acne. Acne is a skin disease common in adolescents that is characterized by the formation of pimples. Excessive rubbing and washing can irritate acne lesions and cause permanent scars.

OCD can also affect a person's diet, leading to health problems linked to poor nutrition. Obsessions associated with scrupulosity, contamination, and the fear of being harmed or harming others often give rise to rigid food-related rituals. These include compulsive behaviors involving portion size, chewing (such as having to chew food a set number of times to prevent harm), food preparation and handling, dietary restrictions, and avoidance of certain foods. Inadequate nutrition can cause unhealthy weight loss and overwhelming fatigue and can compromise the body's ability to fight disease, among other problems. According to Steven D. Tsao, clinic coordinator at the Center for the Treatment and Study of Anxiety at the University of Pennsylvania,

> "It is not uncommon for people with OCD to have symptoms that interfere with their weight, eating, or activity level."[44]
>
> —Steven D. Tsao, clinic coordinator at the Center for the Treatment and Study of Anxiety at the University of Pennsylvania

> It is not uncommon for people with OCD to have symptoms that interfere with their weight, eating, or activity level. In my work with OCD, I've seen people who are excessively fearful of choking on particular types of food or vomiting after eating foods with particular textures. Some people avoid mixing certain foods or limit the kinds of food they eat at particular times. OCD patients with contamination fears struggle to find foods that feel "clean" or "safe" to buy, store, touch, or eat. These OCD symptoms often lead to limited food choices and significant weight loss.[44]

In fact, it is not uncommon for teens with OCD to also have an eating disorder. Eating disorders involve an obsession with body weight and are especially prevalent in young women. Although there is no proof that one condition triggers the other, research suggests that women who develop OCD as children are at a greater risk of developing an eating disorder in their teens than women without OCD or those with late-onset OCD. Scientists do not know why this is so.

Lack of Sleep

Health problems associated with insufficient sleep and sleep disruption are another challenge many individuals with OCD face. It is difficult for people with OCD to clear their minds of obsessions, which makes it hard for them to fall asleep. Others do not get sufficient sleep because they spend so much time before going to bed performing checking rituals. One example is seventeen-year-old Sophie. "[Instead of going to sleep] I would check to make sure all the windows and doors were locked every 10 minutes," she explains. "And if I wasn't checking them I was asking my parents if they were closed and locked. These issues soon escalated into other things, such as going around my house turning off the light switches and repeating these over and over again—on, off, on, off. . . . I was unable to settle down to sleep with these worries going through my mind."[45]

Getting sufficient sleep can be especially problematic for teens with OCD. Due to hormonal changes caused by puberty, all teenagers' circadian rhythms, or internal clocks, shift slightly. As a result, it is natural for teens to prefer to go to bed later and wake up later than most adults and children. However, since school and work typically begin in the early morning, this shift means that many teens do not get as much sleep as they need. In addition, many young people use devices with bright lights, such as tablets and cell phones, before going to bed. Research shows that exposure to bright light before bed interferes with sleep.

The combination of normal sleep difficulties and sleep delays connected to OCD makes sleep issues especially challenging for teens with OCD. Lack of sleep can seriously affect how they act and feel during the day, causing problems such as overwhelming fatigue, an inability to concentrate, irritability, and memory loss. It can also increase anxiety, which can worsen OCD symptoms. Likewise, lack of sleep can also compromise the immune system.

Coping

Many teens with OCD take steps to help themselves cope with the challenges they face. One of the most important is educating themselves about OCD. Learning about OCD provides them with valuable information about the disorder and how to deal with it. There are many books, organizations, and websites that offer information. There are also online and local support groups especially for teens with OCD. Support groups allow individuals to share their experiences, provide each other with encouragement, and learn coping strategies.

Teens also get much-needed support by opening up to trusted family members, friends, or a medical professional about their disorder. Keeping OCD a secret is stressful and difficult. And dealing with its challenges alone is an almost unbearable burden. As Katy Herman, a college student with OCD, advises,

> Tell someone you trust what you're feeling, even if in your rational mind your worries seem silly. Look up mental health and counseling resources in your area. Chat privately with your physician next time you go to the doctor and let them know you are struggling a little with mental health. Next, don't worry about the stigma around mental health. Millions and millions of people struggle with some sort of emotional or mental disability. . . . It's not something that most people these days will judge you for. Once people understand the truth about mental health issues—the fact that they're chemical, there's no on-and-off switch, and that it's more complex than being a germaphobe or simply nervous—they are, in my experience, very accepting. So educate yourself and those around you, and find someone to talk to.[46]

Sharing information about their condition with teachers and school personnel is another measure that helps teens with OCD manage their lives. Working together with their teachers, parents, and school counselors can help teens with OCD ensure that they get the best education possible. In addition, two federal laws—the Individuals with Disabilities Education Act and section 504 of the National Rehabilitation Act—help and support many young people with OCD at school. These acts mandate that students with disabilities receive an education that is equal to that of nondisabled students and meets their individual educational needs. For instance, teachers may allot teens with OCD extra time to complete assignments, modify assignments, or make other accommodations to help them succeed academically. Gail, a parent of a teenager with OCD, comments,

> When my daughter was diagnosed with OCD at age 13, I knew it was critical that her teachers be aware of her condition. So, each year we had a knowledgeable individual meet with her core teachers to explain what OCD is, and specifically review how her symptoms impact her learning. . . . Every year the teachers would express their gratitude because the session allowed them to improve their ability to teach my daughter. They would make the adjustments that were necessary—extended time on tests, reducing the number of math problems for homework, or privately answering questions after class if she had been distracted during a lecture—all in an effort to help her succeed in school.[47]

Practicing stress-reduction techniques also helps teens with OCD gain control of their lives. Stress increases anxiety and may cause OCD symptoms to worsen in vulnerable teens. One way teens counter stress is through exercise. Exercising for at least thirty minutes at a time causes the brain to release endorphins, which are chemicals that provide individuals with a feeling of overall well-being. Exercising also helps teens to redirect their thoughts. Activities like yoga or tai chi, which emphasize focusing the mind, are particularly helpful in reducing anxiety and promoting calm. Listening to soothing music, working on a hobby, or keeping a journal can increase a teen's level of serenity too.

These and other steps help teens with OCD cope. In fact, most teens with OCD go on to live productive, happy lives. However, the challenges they face along the way can be daunting. As St. John writes, "There is nothing you cannot do if you have OCD. This could also be said vice versa; you could also lose your entire life to OCD. To prevent this from happening, you must make all the necessary effort to defeat OCD." [48]

CHAPTER FOUR

Can OCD Be Treated or Cured?

Currently there is no cure for OCD. However, treating the disorder can significantly reduce or even eliminate OCD symptoms, which is why teens and others with the disorder should not wait to seek help. As Katy Herman, a college student with OCD, relates, "I consider myself to be really lucky, because I was diagnosed with OCD very early in my life and my parents were instantly willing and able to set me up with medication and therapy. . . . Thanks in large part to all of the help I've gotten, and a lot of effort on my own part, I'm doing really well."[49]

Diagnosing OCD

The first step toward recovery is getting an accurate diagnosis. Diagnosing OCD is not easy. There are no medical tests that can detect the disorder. Health care professionals rely on a variety of assessment tools to determine whether patients meet criteria set down by the American Psychiatric Association's *Diagnostic and Statistical Manual of Mental Disorders* for identifying and diagnosing OCD. Since not all health care professionals are knowledgeable about the diagnosis and treatment of OCD, it is best to seek help from a mental health professional, such as a psychiatrist, psychologist, or mental health counselor, who is specially trained and experienced in working with OCD patients. Finding a knowledgeable professional is important because OCD can be confused with other mental disorders with similar symptoms. These include general anxiety disorder, attention-deficit/hyperactivity disorder, eating disorders, and Tourette's syndrome, among others. To help patients connect with qualified pro-fessionals, the International OCD Foundation's website maintains an up-to-date listing of OCD special-ists throughout the world.

In order to make an accurate di-agnosis, mental health profession-als conduct a clinical interview with the patient. Patients are questioned about their behavioral history, ob-sessions, compulsive behaviors, and overall well-being. Many teens are so embarrassed by their ob-sessions and compulsive acts that they are reluctant to discuss them with anyone, even a mental health professional. However, therapists are neither judgmental nor easily shocked by anything a patient says. It is important that teens are open with the therapist about their problems so that they can get the help they need. Josh Steinberg, a high school student whose OCD symptoms have been reduced through treatment, advises other teens that

> "I consider myself to be really lucky, because I was diagnosed with OCD very early in my life and my parents were instantly willing and able to set me up with medication and therapy. . . . Thanks in large part to all of the help I've gotten, and a lot of effort on my own part, I'm doing really well."[49]
>
> —Katy Herman, a college student with OCD

> it can be helpful to think of OCD as a net that catches—and won't release—your most random thoughts. Some thoughts can be scary because they involve death or sexual things; however, it's important to remember that all people have these thoughts. You are—and I was—different because your net is not letting these thoughts pass through like other people can do. Don't be ashamed of your thoughts. Share them with those who can help you.[50]

In addition to an oral interview, therapists use a tool known as the Yale-Brown Obsessive Compulsive Scale (Y-BOCS) and Symptoms Checklist to identify a patient's obsessional themes and compulsive behaviors and determine the severity of the OCD.

It consists of a list of more than sixty obsessions and compulsive acts. Patients check off whichever obsessions and compulsive behaviors relate to their particular condition. Then, using a numerical scale, they rate the level of anxiety each symptom causes them. Health care professionals use the results to design a treatment plan that suits the patient's specific needs.

Getting Help with Exposure and Response Prevention Therapy

Once teens and others are diagnosed with OCD, treatment can begin. OCD treatment typically involves a type of cognitive behavioral therapy (CBT) known as exposure and response prevention therapy (ERPT or ERP). CBT is based on the theory that a person's thoughts, emotions, and behaviors are linked and that the way people interpret their thoughts affects the way they feel and behave. Therefore, when teens with OCD change the way they interpret their thoughts, they can reduce feelings of fear and anxiety and prevent themselves from performing compulsive rituals.

"You want to give a person some new experiences with the things that make them anxious and in that experience comes a new understanding about it."[51]

—Jeff Szymanski, the executive director of the International OCD Foundation, a clinical associate at McLean Hospital's OCD Institute, and a clinical instructor in psychology at Harvard Medical School

ERPT is one of the most effective types of CBT for treating OCD. In ERPT, patients make a conscious choice to be exposed to and confront their fears without doing the accompanying compulsive ritual that these fears provoke. Over time patients learn that they can be in a fearful situation without anything bad occurring, and they do not need to perform compulsive rituals to reduce their distress or protect themselves. Jeff Szymanski, the executive director of the International OCD Foundation, explains that "you want to give a person some new experiences with the things that make them anxious and in that experience comes a new understanding about it."[51]

The therapy consists of two parts: exposure and response prevention. The exposure component consists of patients confronting their fear either physically or mentally and staying exposed until their anxiety level decreases at least by half. The response prevention part of the treatment involves resisting the need to perform compulsive rituals in response to the exposures. For example, a teenager with a fear of germs might be instructed to shake the therapist's hand and stay in the situation until the teen's anxiety level lessens naturally without the teen performing a compulsive ritual like hand washing immediately thereafter. In each subsequent session, the teen is instructed to wait longer and longer before washing up, until the teen becomes accustomed to shaking hands without needing to do a compulsive ritual to feel better.

A young woman shares her feelings and fears during a counseling session. OCD cannot be cured, but it can be diagnosed and managed with help from a trained mental health professional.

Once the teen has overcome this fear, the process is repeated with another fear. Exposures are experienced in a hierarchy based on the results of the Y-BOCS Symptoms Checklist. Patients gradually work their way up from moderately stressful thoughts and situations to those that cause them the most distress. So, if the teen gave handshaking an anxiety rating of ten, the next challenge might involve doing something that the teen rated a twenty, such as touching a doorknob, and so on until the teen overcomes his or her greatest fear. As a result, the teen's thoughts and behaviors concerning germs gradually change on their own. In medical terms, this process is known as habituation, and it involves the lessening of a physical or emotional response to a frequently repeated stimulus. According to OCD expert Patrick B. McGrath, "ERP works by having people do what they fear, stay in the situation until they are no longer anxious or have reduced their anxiety level by half, and realize that just because they experience fear does not mean that anything bad will happen to them. Doing ERP can decrease compulsive behaviors by both inhibiting rituals and challenging the validity of obsessional thoughts."[52]

> "ERP works by having people do what they fear, stay in the situation until they are no longer anxious or have reduced their anxiety level by half, and realize that just because they experience fear does not mean that anything bad will happen to them."[52]
>
> —Patrick B. McGrath, director of the OCD and Related Anxiety Disorders Program at the Alexian Brothers Behavioral Health Hospital in Hoffman Estates, Illinois

Difficult and Effective

ERPT is not easy. Although the process may not sound scary to individuals that do not suffer from OCD, for teens and others with the disorder, ERPT is extremely challenging. To the OCD mind, experiencing an exposure is the equivalent of voluntarily putting oneself in danger, which may be why approximately 25 percent of OCD patients either refuse the treatment or fail to complete it. As an eighteen-year-old blogger with OCD writes,

OCD is a very real thing to the person suffering from it because their brain is telling them it's the way things are around them. . . . Think of the one thing that scares you the most . . . and imagine that you have to face that fear. For instance, if you were scared of spiders, you would start out sitting in a room with a spider and gradually work your way to having a spider on your body! It sounds almost impossible to the person with the fear, but people who like spiders can't imagine why being around a spider would be such a big deal.[53]

The Exposure Hierarchy

Using an exposure hierarchy helps prevent patients from feeling overwhelmed by ERPT. An exposure hierarchy is a list of a person's anxiety-provoking situations rated from zero to one hundred based on the amount of distress each situation or thought causes. Working on low-rated exposures first and gradually working up to more fearful situations helps give patients the confidence they need to successfully complete ERPT. Montreal psychologist Danny Gagnon compares the hierarchy to a ladder: "Imagine that you were asked to climb over a 10-foot wall. Would you be able to? Would you have confidence in your ability to do so? But if you were provided with a ladder, you could climb up one step at a time until you were able to climb over the wall. Now would this be useful? Would you have confidence in your ability?"

Moreover, patients and therapists often use the hierarchy concept to break down individual fears into smaller parts. As Gagnon explains,

Sometimes a situation may [be] too difficult to enter because it is too anxiety provoking. If this is the case, you can simply create an exposure hierarchy for that one situation. For example, if taking the elevator elicits 100% anxiety, you can create an exposure hierarchy for this single situation such as: standing in front of the elevator, then getting on the elevator and going up one floor with people, then two floors with others present, then go up one floor alone, then two floors alone, etc.

Danny Gagnon, "Facing Your Fears: How to Successfully Perform Exposure Therapy." www.montrealcbt psychologist.com.

A typical course of ERPT lasts about four months. Therapy sessions take up to three hours per session and are held at least twice a week. In addition, patients must commit to practicing exposures at home too. The more often a patient does a particular exposure, the more likely that the patient will become habituated to it. Moreover, even when patients successfully complete ERPT, they need to periodically practice doing exposures in order to keep OCD symptoms from flaring up.

Despite these challenges, many teens who successfully complete ERPT say that it was worth the effort. As the above-cited eighteen-year-old blogger comments, "Speaking from experience, it basically sucks while you're doing it, but it works! It takes a lot of dedication, hard work, and support from loved ones to get through, but once your first fear is accomplished OCD doesn't seem so big. There might not be a cure, but there's definitely hope to live a happy life!"[54]

Teens Have an Advantage

In fact, research suggests that 90 percent of people with OCD experience moderate to total improvement in their symptoms during ERPT treatment, and 70 percent show long-term improvement three years after treatment. One reason why ERPT is so effective is that it retrains the brain. Humans learn through repeated experiences. When people with OCD repeatedly perform rituals in response to anxiety, their behavior becomes ingrained in their brains. By repeatedly practicing new behavior, ERPT helps people with OCD unlearn OCD behaviors and retrain their brains to deal with anxiety in a healthier manner.

Retraining the brain through ERPT therapy may be especially effective during the teen years. Research shows that the brain grows and changes as a result of new experiences. It does this by forming new neural connections or pathways that transmit new learning to different areas of the brain. The more these pathways are used, the stronger they become.

Changing one's thoughts and behavior through ERPT supports the formation of new pathways. As the new pathways strengthen, old pathways associated with OCD are used less.

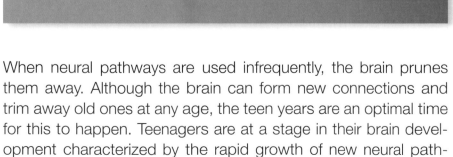

Exposure and response prevention therapy gradually exposes individuals to the things they fear. Little by little they learn that their fears far exceed reality until eventually a person who has an uncontrollable fear of spiders, for instance, can actually hold a spider in his or her hand.

When neural pathways are used infrequently, the brain prunes them away. Although the brain can form new connections and trim away old ones at any age, the teen years are an optimal time for this to happen. Teenagers are at a stage in their brain development characterized by the rapid growth of new neural pathways and the trimming back of less used ones. Therefore, when it

An Herbal Treatment for OCD

For a number of reasons, some people do not care to take SSRI medication. Some of these individuals turn to herbal remedies as a substitute for drug treatment. Herbal remedies use the stems, roots, leaves, bark, and seeds of plants with healing properties to treat a wide range of illnesses. St. John's wort, which is derived from flowers of the St. John's wort plant, is one of the most widely used herbs for treating OCD. It has been used to treat mental disorders for centuries.

A number of studies have been conducted to determine whether the herb can reduce OCD symptoms. The results are mixed. Some studies show a significant improvement in the subjects' symptoms, but other studies do not. Nor is it clear how the herb works. The prevailing theory is that the herb increases the availability of serotonin in the brain, much like SSRI medication.

Herbal treatments are not without risk. Like traditional medication, they can cause unpleasant side effects. Side effects linked to St. John's wort include sleep disturbances, irritability, stomach upset, dry mouth, and headaches. Moreover, unlike conventional medications, herbal remedies are not regulated by the US Food and Drug Administration. As a result, the purity or effectiveness of an herbal treatment may be suspect.

comes to eliminating unwanted pathways associated with obsessions and compulsive behaviors and developing new pathways that relay healthier thoughts and actions, teens have a biological advantage over adults and children.

Medication

Even though teens have an advantage in retraining their brains, ERPT treatment alone may not provide them adequate relief. In these cases, the addition of a selective serotonin reuptake inhibitor (SSRI or SRI) often helps. SSRIs are a class of antidepressant medication that increases serotonin levels in the brain. Numerous studies have found SSRIs to be effective in reducing OCD symptoms. SSRIs lower anxiety, reduce depression, improve mood, and enhance a person's ability to control impulsive actions, which may make it easier for people with OCD to face the challenge of ERPT.

There are a number of different SSRI drugs. Fluoxetine (Prozac), fluvoxamine (Luvox), paroxetine (Paxil), clomipramine (Anafranil), and sertraline (Zoloft) are among the most widely prescribed to treat OCD. Though effective, these drugs are not fast acting. It takes an average of ten to twelve weeks for SSRIs to reduce OCD symptoms, and it is common for patients to have to try different SSRIs and different dosages before finding a combination that works for them. Ray St. John began taking Prozac to help treat his OCD as a freshman in high school. He recalls the doctor telling him, "If Prozac didn't work, then we would try one of the other SSRIs. And, if that one didn't work, then we'd try a third one and so on. We would do this because even though these medications are all in the same category, they act differently in each person."[55]

About two-thirds of OCD patients who are treated with an SSRI experience a reduction in their symptoms. According to psychiatrist and OCD researcher Wayne K. Goodman, "Among those who do improve, the degree of change is meaningful, but it is rarely complete. A person with OCD who has had a good response to an SRI might report that the time occupied by obsessions and compulsion is cut from six to two hours a day. This may allow the individual to return to work or school and resume a relatively normal and fulfilling life."[56]

> "A person with OCD who has had a good response to an SRI might report that the time occupied by obsessions and compulsion is cut from six to two hours a day. This may allow the individual to return to work or school and resume a relatively normal and fulfilling life."[56]
>
> —Wayne K. Goodman, chairman of the Psychiatry Department at the Icahn School of Medicine at Mount Sinai Hospital in New York City and a researcher specializing in OCD

Patients usually take SSRI medication for six months to one year. Stopping the medication abruptly can lead to unpleasant withdrawal symptoms. Therefore, the dosage is gradually tapered off. Unfortunately, the benefits of the drug do not last once SSRI treatment is discontinued, and it is common for relapses to occur. Research suggests that doing behavioral therapy while taking SSRI medication may delay or even prevent a relapse from occurring when the medication is discontinued.

As with all medication, SSRI drugs can cause disagreeable side effects and present health risks. These include, but are not limited to, an upset stomach, daytime drowsiness, dry mouth, and tremors. Side effects usually lessen over time. If they do not, lowering the dosage or switching to another SSRI may help.

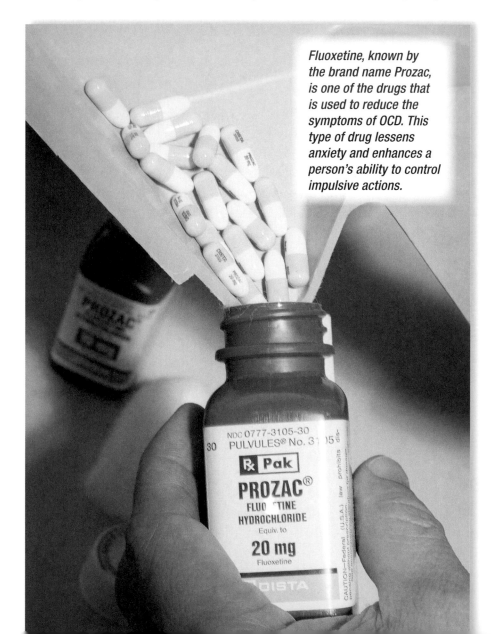

Fluoxetine, known by the brand name Prozac, is one of the drugs that is used to reduce the symptoms of OCD. This type of drug lessens anxiety and enhances a person's ability to control impulsive actions.

Problems for Children and Teens

SSRIs cause additional and more-troubling side effects in some children and teens, but they rarely do so in people over the age of twenty-five. A 2007 review by the US Food and Drug Administration (FDA) of a number of clinical trials involving children and adolescents being treated with SSRIs found that approximately 4 percent of the patients experienced suicidal thoughts or behavior while taking the drugs. This was twice the rate of patients in a control group that were treated with a sugar pill, or placebo. As a result, the FDA requires that the manufacturers of these drugs issue a so-called black box warning on the medication packaging, similar to the warning on cigarette packages, indicating that these drugs may increase suicide risk in children and adolescents. According to the NIMH, "The warning also notes that children and adolescents taking SSRI medications should be closely monitored for any worsening in depression, emergence of suicidal thinking or behavior, or unusual changes in behavior, such as sleeplessness, agitation, or withdrawal from normal social situations."[57] The risk appears to be greatest during the first four weeks of treatment and then appears to diminish. Consequently, close monitoring of young patients is important during this time.

Most young people who take SSRIs do not develop abnormal behavior. Scientists do not know why the drugs elicit suicidal thoughts in some young people and are conducting studies in an effort to learn more. Meanwhile, many mental health professionals and teens with OCD feel that the benefits of SSRIs outweigh the risks, especially when they are combined with behavioral therapy.

Residential Treatment

One way to ensure that teens with OCD are closely monitored at the onset of SSRI treatment is through a residential treatment program. Such programs require patients to live at a special treatment facility for one to three months. There they receive intensive treatment in a highly controlled environment. Patients undergo daily ERPT therapy sessions. The controlled environment offers teens and others additional support while making it more difficult for them to succumb to their compulsive behaviors. For instance, access to hand washing or showers may be monitored and limited. For some individuals, this type of assistance makes ERPT less daunting. Patients also attend group and individual talk therapy sessions, peer-to-peer support group meetings, and educational gatherings in which attendees learn ways to cope with OCD. At the same time, their dosage and response to medication is closely monitored by mental health professionals who are available day and night to handle any crisis that might arise.

Residential treatment is especially helpful for patients who have been unable to face or get through ERPT treatment in the past. Unlike a traditional hospital environment, most residential treatment centers are homey places. Many specialize in working with adolescents. Some adolescent treatment centers also provide an academic program so that teens do not fall behind in their studies while receiving treatment. Others require that teens take time off from school to focus solely on recovering from OCD. Morgan, a young woman with OCD, took a semester off from college to enter residential treatment. She comments,

> After two years of barely treated OCD + college not working . . . I decided to take a semester off from school. I flew myself to a residential OCD treatment center and lived there for nine weeks. This treatment involved four hours of ERP and two psychoeducation groups a day, plus meeting with my therapist three times a week. I spent my time facing some of my most deeply ingrained fears. . . . I am very grateful that I had this opportunity to go through such intensive treatment.[58]

Surgical Procedures

Although most individuals with OCD respond well to CBT and medication, some severe cases do not improve with standard treatment. These individuals have what is known as treatment-resistant or refractory OCD. Neurosurgery provides these people with another treatment option. Neurosurgery for OCD is restricted to people for whom all other treatments have failed, and it is usually limited to patients who are at least eighteen years old. In extremely severe cases, however, neurosurgery may be performed on adolescents. As Christer Lindquist, a neurosurgeon and pioneer in a type of OCD surgery known as gamma knife surgery, explains, "One of our first patients, just 17 years old, was brought to us in a wheelchair. This boy would set himself math problems, which he had to solve before he could eat. His OCD had become so severe, and the math problems he set himself so complex, that he couldn't solve them anymore, so he couldn't eat."[59]

Gamma knife surgery is a form of noninvasive brain surgery in which a neurosurgeon directs thin beams of radiation to a targeted area of the patient's cerebral cortex, which contains neural pathways thought to be involved in OCD. The beams damage a small amount of brain tissue in the targeted area, causing a lesion to develop. The lesion inhibits activity in the targeted pathways, thereby lessening OCD symptoms. According to Antonio Lopes, a neurosurgeon who conducted a clinical trial studying the effects of the surgery, "In people with OCD, the network of areas that communicate is always working, working, working. Medication and behavioral therapy can lower the activity of this brain circuitry. But some people don't respond, and we use the gamma knife to try to cut the connection."[60]

Deep brain stimulation is another type of neurosurgery used to treat resistant OCD. It is more invasive than gamma knife surgery, but it does not destroy any brain tissue. In this procedure, a neurosurgeon drills a hole in the patient's skull and places electrodes in an area of the brain associated with OCD. The electrodes are connected by wires to a tiny device similar to a pacemaker that is implanted in the patient's chest. The device continuously sends an electrical pulse to the electrodes.

About 60 percent of patients who undergo deep brain stimulation surgery report a reduction in OCD symptoms. It is not known why it works. One theory is that the electrical pulse stimulates areas of the brain associated with OCD so that they can work normally. As with all surgeries, both deep brain stimulation and gamma knife surgery are not without risk. However, for people with treatment-resistant OCD, they provide a source of hope.

Future Outlook

It is clear that treating OCD is not easy. Scientists throughout the world are working hard to learn more about the disorder so that they can develop additional treatment options and, possibly, a cure for the condition. In the meantime, many teens with OCD find relief through existing treatments. Indeed, with the right treatment, teens with OCD can take control of the disorder so that they can live happy, productive lives.

Introduction: A Misunderstood Disorder

1. Morgan, "Mental Health Monologues 2015," *My OCD Voice* (blog), April 4, 2016. https://myocdvoice.wordpress.com.
2. Mayo Clinic Staff, "Obsessive-Compulsive Disorder (OCD)," Mayo Clinic. www.mayoclinic.org.
3. Morgan, "Mental Health Monologues 2015."
4. Ray St. John, *The Ray of Hope*. Manville, IL: Vermilion, 2011, p. 97.
5. Alison Dotson, *Being Me with OCD*. Minneapolis: Free Spirit, 2014, p. 3.
6. Quoted in Dotson, *Being Me with OCD,* pp.101–102.

Chapter One: What Is OCD?

7. Patrick B. McGrath, *The OCD Answer Book*. Naperville, IL: SourceBooks, 2007, p. 4.
8. Quoted in Bud Clayman, "Defining OCD," OC87 Recovery Diaries. http://oc87recoverydiaries.com.
9. Samantha Gluck, "What Is OCD?," HealthyPlace.com. www.healthyplace.com.
10. Stan Kutcher, "OCD," *TeenMentalHealth Speaks*. http://teen mentalhealth.org.
11. Quoted in Samantha Gluck, "Clare," HealthyPlace.com, January 20, 2013. www.healthyplace.com.
12. Jennifer Traig, *Devil in the Details*. New York: Back Bay/Little, Brown, 2004, pp. 26–27.
13. Quoted in Dotson, *Being Me with OCD,* p. 29.
14. Jared Douglas Kant, *The Thought That Counts*. New York: Oxford University Press, 2008, p. 13.
15. Kant, *The Thought That Counts,* p. 13.
16. Traig, *Devil in the Details,* p. 4.

17. Joe Wells, *Touch and Go Joe.* London: Jessica Kingsley, 2006, p. 42.
18. Shayla Schoeneberger, "OCD: A Disorder That Is Always with Me," Odyssey, February 1, 2016. www.theodysseyonline.com.
19. St. John, *The Ray of Hope,* p. 34.
20. OCD Center of Los Angeles, "Reassurance Seeking in OCD and Anxiety," February 2, 2010. http://ocdla.com.

Chapter Two: What Causes OCD?
21. OCD-UK, "What Causes OCD?" www.ocduk.org.
22. KidsHealth, "Obsessive-Compulsive Disorder," February 2012. http://kidshealth.org.
23. Quoted in Johns Hopkins Medicine, "Researchers Identify Genetic Marker Linked to OCD," May 13, 2014. www.hopkins medicine.org.
24. Quoted in Weill Cornell Medical College, "Weill Cornell Researchers Find That a Single Gene Is Responsible for OCD-like Behaviors in Mice," April 25, 2010. http://weill.cornell.edu.
25. National Institute of Mental Health, "PANDAS: Fact Sheet About Pediatric Autoimmune Neuropsychiatric Disorders Associated with Streptococcal Infections." www.nimh.nih.gov.
26. National Institute of Mental Health, "PANDAS."
27. International OCD Foundation, "Sudden and Severe Onset OCD (PANS/PANDAS)—Practical Advice for Practitioners and Parents." https://iocdf.org.
28. Quoted in Weill Cornell Medical School, "Learning to Overcome Fear Is Difficult for Teens," September 27, 2012. http://weill.cornell.edu.
29. Janet Singer, "A Perfect Storm?," *OCD Talk* (blog), February 27, 2011. https://ocdtalk.wordpress.com.

Chapter Three: What Is It Like to Live with OCD?
30. Schoeneberger, "OCD."
31. Stan Kutcher, *How Do I Teen My Parent?,* TeenMentalHealth.org. http://teenmentalhealth.org.

32. Emily Shapiro, "What's It Really Like to Live with OCD?," Odyssey, March 7, 2016. www.theodysseyonline.com.

33. Kant, *The Thought That Counts,* pp. 59–60.

34. Quoted in Henry L Gravitz, *Obsessive-Compulsive Disorder: New Help for the Family*. 2nd ed. Santa Barbara, CA: Healing Vision, 2005, p. 15.

35. Quoted in Alison Dotson, "Tuesday Q & A: Gail Bernstein," January 19, 2016. https://alisondotson.com.

36. St. John, *The Ray of Hope,* p. 93.

37. St. John, *The Ray of Hope*, pp. 36–37.

38. Traig, *Devil in the Details,* p. 236.

39. Wells, *Touch and Go Joe,* p. 27.

40. Quoted in Alison Dotson, "A Round-Up of Advice," October 12, 2015. https://alisondotson.com.

41. Jill Armstrong, "I Embrace You OCD," Beyond OCD. http://beyondocd.org.

42. Dotson, *Being Me with OCD,* p. 13.

43. Ross Bonander, "The Effects of Compulsive Hand-Washing," BrainPhysics.com, December 27, 2012. www.brainphysics.com.

44. Steven D. Tsao, "OCD and Eating Disorders: Untangling the Diagnostic Web," Beyond OCD. http://beyondocd.org.

45. Quoted in Dotson, *Being Me with OCD,* pp. 30–31.

46. Katy Herman, "Speak Out: How I Deal with OCD and Anxiety," Beyond OCD, July 16, 2015. http://beyondocd.org.

47. Gail S., "Educating the Educators About OCD," OCD Education Station. www.ocdeducationstation.org.

48. St. John, *The Ray of Hope,* p. 49.

Chapter Four: Can OCD Be Treated or Cured?

49. Herman, "Speak Out."

50. Josh Steinberg, "Guest Post—Teen Talk: One Teen's Guide to Conquering OCD," International OCD Foundation, April 21, 2016. https://iocdf.org.

51. Quoted in Susan Donaldson James, "Why Lena Dunham Can't Just Talk Her Way Out of OCD," NBC News, September 8, 2014. www.nbcnews.com.

52. McGrath, *The OCD Answer Book*, p. 132.
53. *Life with OCD* (blog), "CBT Sucks . . . but It Works!," March 26, 2010. http://ocdteen.blogspot.com.
54. *Life with OCD*, "CBT Sucks . . . but It Works!"
55. St. John, *The Ray of Hope,* p. 110.
56. Wayne K. Goodman, "Medications for OCD," PsychCentral, 2015. http://psychcentral.com.
57. National Institute of Mental Health, "Antidepressant Medications for Children and Adolescents: Information for Parents and Caregivers." www.nimh.nih.gov.
58. Morgan Rondinelli, "Who Am I? A Student with OCD and Anxiety," OC87 Recovery Diaries, 2016. http://oc87recovery diaries.com.
59. Quoted in Lucy Atkins, "A Radical Treatment for Obsessive-Compulsive Disorder Patients," *Guardian* (Manchester, UK), December 14, 2009. www.theguardian.com.
60. Quoted in Charlene Laino, "High-Tech Procedure 'Cuts' Abnormal Brain Wiring Linked to Obsessive-Compulsive Disorder," WebMD, May 8, 2008. www.webmd.com.

RECOGNIZING SIGNS OF TROUBLE

Common Symptoms of OCD
- Having repeated, distressful, unwanted thoughts or images that individuals cannot control
- Having excessive concern with germs, dirt, or contamination
- Having excessive concern with symmetry and order
- Having excessive fear of violating religious rules
- Having excessive fear of discarding unwanted items
- Having excessive feelings of doubt and uncertainty
- Having excessive concern with perfection
- Having fears related to numbers
- Having persistent anxiety
- Having a persistent need for reassurance and/or approval
- Having persistent and distressing sexual thoughts
- Having persistent and distressing violent thoughts
- Having persistent fear of causing oneself or others harm
- Performing rituals to relieve anxiety
- Spending at least one hour a day on obsessive thoughts and rituals

The following organizations offer help for teens and others suffering from OCD, as well as detailed information about this disorder.

American Academy of Child and Adolescent Psychiatry (AACAP)

3615 Washington Ave. NW
Washington, DC 20016-3007
website: www.aacap.org

The AACAP works to educate the public about issues affecting the mental health of children and adolescents. A topic search on the website produces many articles about OCD.

American Psychological Association (APA)

750 First St. NE
Washington, DC 20002-4242
website: www.apa.org

The APA is a professional association representing psychologists. A search on its website yields a variety of information about OCD.

Anxiety and Depression Association of America (ADAA)

8701 Georgia Ave., Suite 412
Silver Spring, MD 20910
website: www.adaa.org

The ADAA offers information about depression and various anxiety disorders, including OCD. It has special sections for college students and adolescents on its website. It also helps people locate therapists, support groups, and mental health apps.

Association for Behavioral and Cognitive Therapies (ABCT)

305 Seventh Ave., 16th Fl.
New York, NY 10001
website: www.abct.org

The ABCT is an organization dedicated to advancing mental health treatment through the use of behavioral therapies. It provides articles, podcasts, and videos related to the treatment of various mental disorders, including OCD, on its website.

Beyond OCD

2300 Lincoln Park West, Suite 206B
Chicago, IL 60614
website: www.beyondocd.org

This organization is dedicated to helping people with OCD cope. It provides a wealth of information and publications, personal stories, and a special section for teens on its website.

International OCD Foundation

PO Box 961029
Boston, MA 02196
website: https://iocdf.org

This organization's mission is to raise public awareness about OCD. It offers fact sheets, articles, and a directory of qualified therapists on its website. There is also a special section aimed at helping families cope with the disorder.

National Alliance on Mental Illness (NAMI)

3803 N. Fairfax Dr., Suite 100
Arlington, VA 22203
help line: (800) 950-6264
website: www.nami.org

NAMI is a large organization working to improve the lives of people with mental illness and their families. There is information about numerous mental disorders on its website, including OCD, and a special section for teens and young adults.

National Institute of Mental Health (NIMH)

6001 Executive Blvd., Room 8184, MSC 9663
Bethesda, MD 20892-9663
website: www.nimh.nih.gov

The NIMH is a federal agency that provides information on mental disorders. It also sponsors and conducts research related to mental disorders. A search on its website produces numerous articles about OCD.

Books

Shirley Brinkerhoff, *Obsessive-Compulsive Disorder*. New York: Mason Crest, 2014.

Alison Dotson, *Being Me with OCD*. Minneapolis: Free Spirit, 2014.

Jonathan Grayson, *Freedom from Obsessive-Compulsive Disorder*. New York: Berkley, 2014.

H.W. Poole, *Obsessive-Compulsive Disorders*. New York: Mason Crest, 2016.

Leslie J. Shapiro, *Understanding OCD*. Santa Barbara, CA: Praeger, 2015.

Internet Sources

HealthyPlace.com, "OCD and Related Disorders." www.healthy place.com/ocd-related-disorders.

Owen Kelly, "10 Facts About Obsessive-Compulsive Disorder," VeryWell, June 29, 2016. www.verywell.com/top-ocd-facts-25 10674.

KidsHealth, "Obsessive Compulsive Disorder." http://kidshealth .org/en/teens/ocd.html.

OCD Chicago, *Got OCD? A Guide for Teens,* Beyond OCD, 2009. http://beyondocd.org/uploads/pdf/got-ocd.pdf.

OCD Education Station, "OCD Facts," 2016. www.ocdeduca tionstation.org/ocd-facts.

Traci Petersen, "New Insights into Genetics of OCD and Tourette's Syndrome," PsychCentral, October 26, 2013. http://psychcen tral.com/news/2013/10/26/new-insights-into-genetics-of-ocd -tourette-syndrome/61203.html.

INDEX

*Note: Boldface page numbers
indicate illustrations.*

PICTURE CREDITS

Barbara Sheen is the author of ninety-four nonfiction books for young people. She lives in New Mexico with her family. In her spare time, she likes to swim, garden, cook, and walk.